Alkali1

Supercharge Your Body & Mind, Speed Up Natural Weight Loss, and Enjoy Vibrant Energy

By Marta Tuchowska

www.HolisticWellnessProject.com

The book is not intended to provide medical advice or to take the place of medical advice and treatment from your personal physician. Readers are advised to consult their own doctors or other qualified health professionals regarding the treatment of medical conditions. The author shall not be held liable or responsible for any misunderstanding or misuse of the information contained in this book. The information is not intended to diagnose, treat or cure any disease.

Contents

INTRODUCTION- REVOLUTIONIZE YOUR HEALTH WITH ALKALINE JUICING

Are you looking for a natural way to revolutionize your health and feel amazing?

If the answer is "yes", you have come to the right place!
I would like to welcome you to the **World of Alkaline Juicing**. It's a vibrant health zone where our focus is on nourishing our bodies and minds with colorful and energizing nutrients.

Before we jump into the recipes, this book's focus, we will explore the benefits of juicing and then briefly have a look at the benefits of alkaline juicing, foods, and lifestyle in general. I will also add a few words of caution to help you avoid unnecessary confusion about juicing and alkaline diets.

The word "alkaline" has recently become a catchy marketing phrase (just like "Paleo" or "vegan" or even "gluten-free") and a popular diet "hashtag". This means there is lots of conflicting information available. This information is very often passed on by people who have never lived any of the above-mentioned lifestyles nor done any thorough research. This is why, it's not uncommon to encounter lots of skepticism around the alkaline diet and other diets as well.

Don't get me wrong, I totally respect all kinds of healthy modern clean diets (including Paleo, vegan, alkaline, gluten-free, macrobiotic), but we need to fully understand how they all work and ultimately, create something that works for us.

Everyone is different and their personalized diets and lifestyles should be as well. I am very open minded to all kinds of nutritional approaches, and at the same time, I am a big believer in Alkalinity.

The reasons I wrote this book were:

1. I want to motivate you to add more fresh, alkaline juices into your diet.
2. I want to provide you with the best of my recipes so alkaline juicing becomes your lifestyle, regardless of the diet you decided to follow.
3. I want to teach you which foods are alkaline-forming and which are not. The information I share is very easy to understand and to apply. After going through this book, you will know exactly what to do and how to combine intuition with science and your personal preferences (it's not about trying to "force yourself" to

eat and drink something you can't stand, it's all about understanding the Big Picture!).

Small actions and consistency lead to massive transformations.

PART I THE BENEFITS OF JUICING

Why Juicing?

The question I very often get is: "why should one consider juicing when these vegetables can always be cooked or even eaten raw? Does juicing make any difference?"

The answer is very simple:

1. In the process of cooking, especially over-cooking, we lose many vital nutrients and enzymes.

2. At the same time, if you go for too many raw foods, there is every possibility that your body's natural digestion won't efficiently break them down (there is a limit to how much fiber we can handle). How long does it take to eat a massive salad?

Don't get me wrong, I love my salads just like I love some healthy cooked meals. It's great to have them as a healthy foundation. But...there is something more we can do to fully revolutionize our health and enjoy more energy. Start juicing on top of a healthy, clean-food diet. This is a balanced, common-sense and realistic approach. A very simple decision that can really improve your wellbeing.

Yes, eating heaps of veggies can be time-consuming or even unrealistic. You can eliminate all these problems and revolutionize your health by juicing some of your veggies. Besides, would it be possible to eat all those heaps of fruits and vegetables? Probably not. There would be a limit.

While I love snacking on some raw veggies, or making delicious colorful salads, I am also a big fan of juicing because it's like a quick injection of energy and nutrients. My mind and body can immediately feel it! If your goal is optimal nutrition and unstoppable energy- juicing is the way.

Moreover, juicing your vegetables offers a great convenience to you if you detest the taste of some of them (not everyone is mad about spinach or kale). Considering the fact that juicing has to do with gulping the juice rather than chewing it, it's so much easier. I have worked with people who had a really hard time adding veggies to their diets. They also had a hard time drinking dense green smoothies. But...juicing made it so much easier for them.

Make it, drink it and forget it! It also works great for people who forget to eat their veggies. Well, drinking your veggies and creating amazing, holistic elixirs (the right way, and this guide will show you how) can be the missing ingredient to your super healthy, balanced lifestyle. Maybe you have already been eating healthier and healthier and making significant changes to your diet and now you are wondering-how can I take it to the next level? Well, this book will show you how.

Maybe, you are just getting started on your journey? Well, through the following pages you will discover a "healthy shortcut" because you will know exactly what to focus on (and you will also avoid my early mistakes with juicing- that alone will save you time, money and frustration).

It's all about well-designed juicing rituals. Alkaline juicing rituals! It's like a shot of health. Once you have mastered the art of alkaline juicing, you will feel confident that every day you are feeling stronger and stronger and getting closer to your wellness goals.

Juicing can be so much healthier and convenient compared to cooking (or better said "over-cooking"), because it will preserve all the nutrients, and present you with a real, natural "energy bomb". Your body will be so grateful, trust me on that one!

Benefits of juicing

The whole idea behind juicing is offer rest to your digestive tract and organs responsible for digestion, energy production, and waste control (kidneys, bladder, colon, liver, intestines), thereby, helping you experience a healthier digestive system. Aside from the actual "rest" for your digestive system, you are also feeding your body with a myriad of nutrients to help your body heal and feel amazing.

When you juice your foods, you actually take all the fibers from it, which leaves room for *instant absorption* of nutrients and faster conversion of food to energy in the blood.
(by the way, you can still keep the fiber and add it to your salads, healthy, plant-based stir-fries, or even healthy, gluten-free baking recipes, if you wish).

When you drink fresh alkaline juices, you will have more stamina and energy in your body, simply, because the body will utilize the saved energy derived from digestion and conversion of food to blood sugar. Almost 30% of the energy in the body can be used for other activities. Fresh, alkaline juice is the best natural coffee for your body and mind. And it truly has the power to revitalize all the systems your body needs to pay you back with vibrant health.

The fact that nutrients are quickly absorbed means they are quickly distributed to cells, thereby aiding healing and repairs. Antioxidants derived from alkaline foods that are easily accessible have the potential to swiftly reduce damage brought about by blood radicals and also lessen the risk of many preventable diseases.

Juicing for Weight Loss?

I very often get asked if juicing can help with weight loss. The answer is yes. This is definitely the number 1 tip I would give if you want to lose weight, naturally and in a healthy, sustainable way. Even if you are happy with your current weight, juicing will help you maintain it and restore your energy. It's the best anti-age, holistic health and natural weight loss treatment you can get!

Here's why:
-Concentrated Nutrients. You have access to all the essential nutrients required to lose weight in a more intense, but at the same time, natural way. When your body receives an abundance of nutrients it no longer craves unhealthy foods that can make you put on weight. At the same time, your mood and energy levels will improve. A healthy, balanced mind wants a healthy, balanced body. When you start feeling healthy, it's so much easier to take a healthy, inspired action, for example- using that natural energy to go for a walk every evening, joining a yoga class, or work out and actually enjoy it. Hence, losing weight is more effective, because your body feels

well-nourished and energized, and your mind feels inspired and motivated.

It's amazing how one, simple wellness decision- such as enriching your diet and lifestyle with fresh, alkaline juice, can radically transform your body! It's all interconnected.

-Strong Detoxifying Properties. Alkaline juices offer incredible detoxifying properties. By giving your body the nutrients it needs to stay in balance and helping it detox on a deeper level, you get to enjoy vibrant health, massive energy and natural weight loss.

-Less Sugar Cravings. Most people have difficulty losing weight or enjoying a healthy lifestyle due to their failure to control their appetites or sugar cravings. The more we eat/drink something, the more we crave it. For example, if a person lives on processed foods and soda, all they want is more and more of it. To get rid of this "vicious cycle", it's very important to focus on abundance first. I mean- the abundance of nutrients! Alkaline juices are super low in sugar and super high in nutrients. By focusing on adding more alkaline juices into your diet, you will experience less and less of "unhealthy cravings" that could be sabotaging your health success.
For example, try to juice cucumbers, tomatoes, and add in some Himalayan salt and spices. Then, add a splash of olive

oil, and you have a Spanish Gazpacho style juice. It's a really nutritious and alkalizing drink, full of nutrients, vitamins and good fats.

It's all about providing your body with nutrients that it needs to thrive. Do you know why your body craves sugar and crappy, processed carbs? Well, it's telling you that it's not only hungry, but that it needs nutrients. We need to be grateful when our bodies speak to us!

It's not about eating less, it's about eating right. Focus on enriching your diet with a ton of nutrients (alkaline juices, as you already know are an amazing tool to make your journey simple, doable and fun), and the rest will become so much easier.

This is how you will gradually be able to create your healthy roots, and reducing unhealthy foods will not only be easy but also automatic. You will be creating the new, more empowered version of yourself. Everyone around you will start asking you: "so, what have you been doing?". Everyone will want to know your secrets.

By simply drinking one alkaline juice a day, you will be surprised at the benefits of taking vegetables daily. Quick fixes don't work in health. But...focusing on simple, process-oriented actions, such as regular, healthy, alkaline juicing, topped up with a healthy, clean food diet, physical activity, loved-based mindset and holistic self-care will unleash your next level of deep transformation.

The best part? You don't need any fancy ingredients and you don't need to be an experienced health chef. Anyone can unleash the power of alkaline juicing. All I am asking you to focus on is the bigger picture.

"I've only had this book for a short while but find the difference in aches and pains, or lack of them, amazing. I am mixing these recipes with a basic Paleo way of living, the only difference being we don't have so much meat. I am sticking to the recipes without altering them too much until I get a proper feel for it, but if I keep feeling better like this, they won't need tweaking." – Scotty from the UK

When I wrote the first edition of this book, back in 2015, I was already experiencing the positive benefits of the alkaline juicing and I was very passionate about sharing my message with the world.

Now, in 2019, I am experiencing new levels of health, vitality and transformation and so are my readers, clients and subscribers. I always say: "simplicity means wellness".

I also say" simple actions repeated all over again, lead to the next level". Many readers told me that when they first got started on their alkaline journeys, one of their main goals was to lose weight in a healthy, sustainable way.

And they did reach their goals by combining what I teach with their passion and dedication. But now they tell me that after several years of regular juicing and overall healthy, alkaline lifestyle, they feel happier and much more aligned. They feel like a new person, with a new set of habits and inner motivations.

They can now get up early and they don't need to rely on caffeine. And they are happy they are no longer feeling so tired all the time and can finally pursue their passions or spend quality time with their loved ones.

Ask yourself: "Where do I want to be in 5 years from now? What is my wellness vision?".

Why am I saying this? Well, I want you to see the bigger picture. I would love you to use this book for years to come so that you fall in love with alkaline juicing and use it to transform on a deeper level. I am very positive your transformation and healthy actions will inspire those around you so that more and more people start taking care of their wellbeing.

This is my purpose and I am forever grateful for You, the reader.

Now, it's time to learn a little bit about that "alkaline thing" and make it simple, doable and fun. Even if you are an absolute alkaline beginner-no worries, I got you covered. And, if you are already living this lifestyle, the following pages will offer you extra inspiration and tips.

I also offer an Alkaline Wellness email newsletter you can join at no cost at:

www.HolisticWellnessProject.com/alkaline

When you sign up, you will receive instant access to 3 free bonus guides followed by regular updates, tips and recipes.

You will also receive massive discounts on my new books and other offerings:

3 Free Bonus Guides

Join the Alkaline Wellness Newsletter and get your bonuses at:

www.HolisticWellnessProject.com/alkaline

Any problems with your sign up, please email me at:

info@holisticwellnessproject.com

(Oh, and don't worry about spam, I hate it as much as you do and I only send out relevant information to support your journey)

PART II ALKALINE DIET MADE EASY (THE SIMPLE "COMMON-SENSE" APPROACH)

Now that we know why juicing is so awesome, let's briefly explain the concept of Alkalinity and how it can help us juice the right way.

There are many juicing books out there that will tell you to juice fruit rich in sugar (for example kiwi, pineapple, or some sweet exotic, expensive fruit); however, the alkaline diet focuses mostly on *juicing vegetables* and fruit that is **low in sugar** (limes, lemons, grapefruits, pomegranates). Sure, you can add small pieces of other fruits for taste (this can help you make the transition, and I use this strategy in some of my recipes), but fruit rich in sugar should not be juiced. It's better for you if blended (in a smoothie so it is not separated from its fiber) or eaten as a whole fruit (which is a great addition to a healthy, balanced diet- I have nothing against fruit).

This is the number 1 mistake I see people make when getting started on juicing, and I have been guilty of it as well, so I am not judging. Juicing fruit (not all fruit, but fruit rich in sugar; that is non-alkaline fruit) is a recipe for disaster. It's not good for you, and even worse, if you juice specifically to lose weight.

Unfortunately, many companies have built their entire businesses by telling people to drink plenty of fruit juices.

It doesn't matter if you make fruit juices yourself; sugar is sugar (and again, I don't want to be preachy; I have been guilty of this mistake as well). That is why I am a big fan of Alkaline Juicing- the healthiest method of juicing out there, because it focuses on greens, vegetables and low sugar fruit.

We need to remember:
- Research has shown that fructose without fiber (fruit juices, as juicing deprives fruit of its natural fiber) causes absolute havoc in the body (inflammation, acidity, insulin resistance).
-Fruit is not unhealthy in itself; there is no reason to fear fruit. However, most fruit is not alkaline-forming. We can still eat fruit in moderation, as a part of a healthy, balanced diet! Go for in-season and whole, with the fiber intact (add a bit to your smoothies if needed, or enjoy some fruit as a snack here and there if you want).

But...juicing fruit rich in sugar (non-alkaline fruits) is actually acid-forming.

Ok Marta, enough preaching. Don't be so pompous; you have been guilty of juicing fruit as well....

The reason I am so passionate about it, is that I want you to juice the right way, the alkaline way. The simple and also inexpensive way (juicing fancy fruit can get expensive; but luckily, we don't need any).

So, if you want to "alkalize", energize, and restore your energy levels, you need to focus on juicing:
-Vegetables, especially greens, and this book will show you how to make it, not only bearable, but also super tasty and fun.
-Alkaline forming fruits: limes, lemons, grapefruits etc. (remember to sign up for your bonus guides, educational emails and printable charts at: www.holisticwellnessproject.com/alkaline)

The rule number #1- when it comes to alkaline foods and juicing, you always want to focus on low sugar ingredients. Simple.

Alkaline juices are a great, holistic tool to help nourish and revitalize your body to achieve your health goals, so you can be the person you want to be. They are a great way to add more healthy, alkaline foods into your diet that will help you eradicate:

- Lack of energy
- Mental fog
- Excess Weight

Introduction to Alkaline Juicing

It doesn't matter if you are Paleo, vegan, or gluten-free. You can always add more alkaline foods and drinks into your diet, and alkaline juices are the best way to do it. All the recipes from this book are *100% vegan, dairy-free, gluten-free, and soy-free.* I have included a myriad of recipes with different ingredients to make sure I accommodate different nutritional and taste preferences.

Perhaps you suffer from fatigue, aches and pains, and stiffness, or perhaps you would like to lose weight. You've tried to clean up your diet, but for the life of you, you just can't understand what's making you feel worse than you should be feeling.

Perhaps you feel you are simply ageing, and you need to expect to feel not-so-good anymore.

Well, this book offers simple tools and recipes you can apply to give your body the nutrients and nourishment it needs to thrive. Simple actions and consistency can lead to amazing and sustainable results.

THE ALKALINE DIET BEGINNER-FRIENDLY CRASH COURSE

I am sure you have been waiting for this! Since the book has the word "Alkaline" in the title, I am sure you have been expecting me to write a little bit about the pH.

The good news is that it's not as complicated as many gurus want us to believe. In fact, it's pretty common sense, healthy eating knowledge.

The pH of most of our crucial cellular and other body fluids, like blood, is designed to be at a pH of 7.365 which is slightly alkaline.

Luckily, our miraculous body has an intricate system in place to maintain that healthy, slightly alkaline pH level. It's working for us 24/7, to ensure our pH system stays optimally balanced.

An interesting thing is that our body, as long as it is blessed with the gift of life, will continuously keep working to regulate our pH (whether we eat a healthy diet rich in alkaline foods or not).

Introduction to Alkaline Juicing

The problem? It's up to us to make it easier or harder for our body...

We can totally choose what we eat and drink. But...if we focus on unhealthy choices, for example the Standard Western Diet with its overload of sugars, processed carbohydrates, dairy, soda, too many animal products, and fast food we make it more and more difficult for our body to stay in balance.

Some people say, "Oh, but what is the point of eating a healthy diet rich in alkaline unprocessed foods if our body regulates our pH for us?"

Yes, our body regulates our pH for us, no matter what we eat. We can't make our pH higher and higher. You see, this is not the goal of the alkaline diet. We just can't make our blood's pH more alkaline or "higher." Our body tries to work hard for us to help maintain our ideal pH. We can't have a pH of 8 or 9. It's not about magically raising or re-modifying our body's pH level.

The focus of the alkaline diet is to give your body the nourishment and the healing tools that it needs to MAINTAIN that optimal pH almost effortlessly.

This is achieved by taking in healthy, balanced nutrition rich in alkaline foods (you already know these are good for you!) such as:

- unprocessed foods
- naturally gluten-free foods
- yeast-free foods
- dairy-free foods
- sugar-free foods
- wheat-free foods
- foods rich in minerals, vitamins and chlorophyll
-plant-based foods, greens and veggies (juicing is the best tool to do it!)

If we do not support our bodies with healthy, balanced nutrition, we torture them with incredible stress! Yes, when the body has to continually work overtime to detoxify all of the cells and maintain our pH, it finally succumbs to disease.

It still keeps working and balancing...but...it gets weaker and weaker and we no longer get to enjoy the vibrant health and vitality of our dreams. This is when we become much more prone to disease and there's a downward spiral of physical and mental ailments.

Introduction to Alkaline Juicing

Your body can feel tired because of what you've put into it (processed foods, sugar, caffeine, poor quality water, stress, alcohol, yeast, bacteria, tobacco, gluten, drugs, negative emotions). Add to it: pollution and not enough sleep and lack of physical activity.

It makes sense if you attend to the root cause of the problem by implementing a lifestyle rich in alkaline forming foods, you will naturally take care of what plagues you. As soon as you focus on abundance of nutrients, your body starts craving more and more of "real nutrition".

Again- juicing is one of the best tools. I totally understand that some people are not used to eating heaps of veggies, and they need more time to transition to a clean food lifestyle. Well, juicing can make it not only simple, but also doable and fun. Make it, drink it and forget it. Also, some people can't tolerate too much fiber, and because of that they can't drink massive amounts of smoothies. Once again- alkaline juices will be very helpful!

People who have changed their diets to an alkaline diet experience huge benefits, and there are plenty of real-life stories to back it up. I, myself, have witnessed tremendous changes in my own health; the alkaline diet combined with homeopathy, other natural therapies, and lifestyle changes have helped cure my eye of uveitis (inflammation of the uvea, very often caused by autoimmune disorders), which is a serious eye disease that can even result in blindness.

I have also experienced a myriad of other benefits (sustainable weight loss, more energy, better focus, less anxiety). This is why I am writing this book. I want to show you the practical way of adding more "real foods" into your diet, via juicing, so you can FEEL it yourself.

Here is the sad truth: we can't expect to throw junk into our mouths and think our bodies will respond kindly. No amount of fad supplements or even the latest fad super foods will help. Save your money, time, and energy.

The Alkaline Diet Lifestyle is not about strict dieting, calorie counting or eliminating your favorite foods forever. It's about adding more of the good stuff and learning how to make better food choices. Just eat clean and focus on alkaline foods. Ideally, about 70-80% of your diet should be comprised of alkaline foods. The recipes from this book will help you be creative so you can focus on the abundance of alkaline foods. Go for a challenge. Try to have at least one alkaline juice a day. Important: I am not saying you should live on juices. This is not a juice cleanse book. Simply add more alkaline juices into your current diet, as they will help you feel amazing. The more nourished you feel, the less unhealthy food cravings you have. Health attracts health. Go for small changes. Baby steps.

Alkaline Foods & Drinks are for you if:
- You've tried "dieting" to lose weight and didn't like it.
- You'd like to feel healthy and stronger
- You'd like to feel young and energetic again.
- You'd like to improve your skin.
- You'd like to stop being moody and irritated so often.
- You'd like to improve your focus on concentration

Eating a diet rich in alkaline-forming foods supports our body's natural function to heal itself. Our pH cannot be higher than it is naturally designed to be. The alkaline diet is not about "raising your pH" (with pH like 8 we would all be dead!) but it's about helping our body maintain its ideal weight and health by utilizing holistic, alkaline tools like alkaline foods and drinks.

To sum up, the best tip I could give you is to add more alkaline foods into your diet. Juicing is the easiest way to do it. Go for a challenge and have 1 alkaline juice a day (about 1 cup). It's not about going on complicated detoxes or cleanses, and it has got nothing to do with sticking to a strict 100% green alkaline diet.

Never heard of the Alkaline Diet and don't know where to start?

I remember when I first learned about the alkaline diet, I was more than confused and skeptical. I wanted to take action but didn't know how. I would spend endless hours online looking for alkaline-acid charts only to find there was way too much contradictory information out there.

I don't want you to feel confused. I know that your time is valuable and much better spent doing things you love (which by the way is alkaline, and I recommend it in a conclusion chapter of this book). I also really appreciate the fact you took an interest in my work.

This is why I would love to offer you a <u>free, complimentary alkaline guide</u> and **easy alkaline-acid charts** (printable so that you can keep them on your fridge or in your wallet). It will provide a solid foundation to kick-start your alkaline diet success. You will get all the facts explained in plain English, practical alkaline tips, and yummy, recipes, motivational advice, educational emails to help you stay on track, as well as printable charts for quick reference.

3 Free Bonus Guides

Sign up link:

www.holisticwellnessproject.com/alkaline

(if you experience any technical issues with your sign up, please email me:

info@holisticwellnessproject.com)

ALKALINE JUICING- RECOMMENDED BASIC SHOPPING LIST

Opt for fresh and organic fruits and vegetables. Ordering items online may save time, or you may visit your local farmers' market. You can also order more and split with your neighbors and family to cut down costs. When it comes to fruits and vegetables, the fresher they are, the better. You can also start growing your own.

ALKALINE INGREDIENTS

These ingredients are super alkaline. I suggest you make them your priority.

Here's the list of HIGH alkaline foods:

Alkaline Veggies to use in your juicing recipes:
- Beetroot
- Bell Pepper
- Cabbage
- Celery
- Collard/Spring Greens
- Endive
- Garlic
- Ginger

- Lettuce
- Mustard Greens
- Radish
- Red Onion
- Rocket/Arugula
- Spinach and Kale
- Carrot (great to taste, but do not juice it too much as it is richer in sugar)
- Courgette/Zucchini
- Watercress
- Cucumber
- Kale
- Spinach (baby and grown)
- Parsley
- Broccoli

Super Alkaline Fruits:
- Avocado (can't be juiced, but you can blend it into your juice if you want to add some good fats)
- Tomato
- Lemon
- Lime
- Grapefruit
- Pomegranate

Other Alkaline Smoothie Ingredients you might need:

- Herbal teas (cooled down)
- Herbs (basil, cinnamon, coriander, curry, rosemary, mint, thyme...)
- Almond milk
- Coconut water
- Coconut milk

OILS:

Don't forget about oils- these are "good oils":

- Avocado Oil
- Coconut Oil
- Flax Oil
- Udo's Oil
- Olive Oil

Introduction to Alkaline Juicing

Alkaline nuts and seeds for more nutrients in your juices/ smoothies (you can also snack on them while drinking your juice as it will help your body absorb nutrients faster):

- Almonds
- Coconut
- Flax Seeds
- Pumpkin Seeds
- Sesame Seeds
- Sunflower Seeds

You can get printable food lists + bonus guides by signing up for my Alkaline Wellness newsletter:

www.holisticwellnessproject.com/alkaline

3 Free Bonus Guides

JUICING AND JUICERS

I very often get asked about the tools and equipment needed for juicing. Personally, I am a big fan of Omega Juicer, which I have been successfully and happily using for over 5 years now.

To be more specific, the model I am using is Omega - J8226. It's easy to use and clean and excellent quality. Prior to purchasing Omega juicer, I tried several juicers that were much cheaper, but, unfortunately they never lasted long. Eventually, I decided to invest in Omega Juicer and I absolutely love it.

You may also decide to go for another brand, if you do, be sure to go for "slow", "cold-press" and "masticating" options.

As for other tools and resources I use to make my "alkaline health elixirs" (goes beyond the scope of this booklet), I regularly share them on my website in the "resources" section (including my favorite tools, supplements and programs), in case you're interested in optimizing your healthy lifestyle:

www.HolisticWellnessProject.com/resources

PART III ALKALINE JUICING-DELICIOUS RECIPES TO NOURISH YOUR BODY, MIND AND SOUL

Measurements Used in the Recipes

The cup measurement I use is the American Cup measurement.

I also use it for dry ingredients. If you are new to it, let me help you:

If you don't have American Cup measures, just use a metric or imperial liquid measuring jug and fill your jug with your ingredient to the corresponding level. Here's how to go about it:

1 American Cup= 250ml= 8 fl.oz.

For example:

If a recipe calls for 1 cup of spinach, simply place your spinach into your measuring jug until it reaches the 250 ml/8oz mark.

Quite easy, right?

I know that different countries use different measurements and I wanted to make things simple for you. I have also noticed that very often those who are used to American Cup measurements complain about metric measurements and vice versa. However, if you apply what I have just explained, you will find it easy to use both.

Morning Energy Green Coco Juice

This juice will help you start your day with an abundance of energy. Nothing feels better than knowing you are feeding your body with nutrients first thing in the morning. You can also enjoy this juice in the afternoon as quick "pick me up" recipe.

Servings: 1-2

Ingredients:

- 2 cups baby spinach
- 2 small carrots, peeled (unless organic)
- Half inch ginger, peeled
- 1 red bell pepper
- Half fennel bulb
- 1 lemon, peeled
- 1 tablespoon avocado oil
- Pinch of Himalayan salt

Instructions:

1. Wash and chop the greens, carrots, fennel, lemon and bell pepper.
2. Place through the juicer.
3. Pour the juice into a big glass or other utensil of your choice and stir in 1 tablespoon of avocado oil.

4. Add a bit of Himalayan salt to taste.
5. Enjoy and drink to your health!

Avocado Oil Benefits

Avocado oil is high in Omega 6 (Omega-6 fatty acids play a crucial role in brain function) and Lutein, a nutrient that improves eye health and may lower the risk of age-related eye disease.

Avocado oil also enhances the absorption of important nutrients and is great for a healthy-looking skin.
Aside from adding it to my juices and smoothies, I also like to use it as a massage oil, to nourish my skin and as a natural hair conditioner.

Full on Energy Spicy Green Creative Juicooo-Smoothie

Can you juice avocados?

Nope, of course you can't. Just like, you can't juice bananas. But...you can blend them into your alkaline juices to create an incredibly healthy and sensational, thick, "smoothie style" juice.

How you start your day is how you end your day. If you neglect your nutrition early in the morning, your body will kindly remind you by unexpected food cravings (not always healthy and not always convenient, especially if there is no healthy food around). Try this recipe first thing in the morning or even around mid-morning to feel vibrant and energized (and crave good, healthy food!).

Servings: 2-3
Ingredients:
- 2 cups kale leaves
- 2 small carrots, peeled (unless organic)
- 2 garlic cloves, peeled
- 2 zucchinis, peeled
- 2 big tomatoes
- Half avocado, peeled and pitted

- Himalayan salt
- Black pepper
- Curry powder and chili powder to taste
- Olive oil (1 tablespoon)
- Optional: Barley grass powder for optimal nutrition (1-2 teaspoons)

Instructions:

1. Wash and chop the kale, carrots, zucchini, and tomatoes.
2. Place through a juicer. Add garlic cloves.
3. In the meantime, wash, peel, and chop the avocado fruit.
4. Take your juice, add the avocado bites and place through a blender or food processor (I usually use a small hand blender as avocados are super easy to blend).
5. Stir well, adding some Himalayan salt, spices, and olive oil. You can also add some barley grass powder. Experiment with desired consistency. You may even blend in more avocados and create a thick soup or a sauce that you can have with wraps and other dishes.

As I always say, it doesn't matter if you are vegan, vegetarian, paleo, low-curb, or gluten-free- Alkalinity is the key. Focus on adding more alkaline foods into your diet and the rest will fall in place.

Additional Information
Body & Mind Benefits of Barley Grass:

- It contains loads of vital substances.
- It is a natural, rich source of nutrients and phytonutrients to help your body stay in balance
- It is rich in fiber, potassium, folic acid, calcium, and VIT. B1 and B5. Add to it chlorophyll and carotenoids.

How to use it?

Add about 2 teaspoons of raw, organic barley grass powder to 1 cup (about 0.25 liter) of your drink (water, almond milk, coconut milk, juice or smoothie). I also like to add it to my salads.

My favorite way is to mix 2 teaspoons of Barley Grass with 1 cup of almond milk or coconut milk (unsweetened, natural). Add some cinnamon + ginger + some lemon juice, and you have a body and mind nourishing drink. I don't like to mix it with water, but it could be an option too.

You can do it at work or even when traveling. It only takes a few seconds.

Craving something sweet?

The above-mentioned recipe (barley grass with warm almond milk and some spices) will easily help **fight sugar cravings**. You can add stevia for **natural guilt-free sweetness**...yum...

Of course, it is important to choose a quality brand. We want certified organic, gluten-free, chemical-free, non-GMO, No Fillers/Sweeteners etc.

The good thing about **barley grass** is that compared to other "green powders" and super foods, it's relatively inexpensive. To learn more about the supplements and superfoods I am using to optimize your healthy lifestyle, please visit the "resources" section on my website:

www.HolisticWellnessProject.com/resources

Creamy, Anti-Inflammatory Breakfast Delight

This recipe is great if you have a sweet tooth. Why not indulge in it in a healthy way? The alkaline diet is certainly not about feeling hungry, deprived, or going on some kind of weird, detoxes.

You are about to discover how you can combine healing with taste! Yes, this juice is great as a natural drink. It is packed with nutrients, and uses an army of anti-inflammatory agents like cinnamon, nutmeg, chia seeds, and ginger.

Plus, once you have tried it, it actually becomes a treat, and you wonder how you could ever live without it! Try it when you crave something sweet (usually when you crave sweets, your body is trying to tell you that it needs more vital nutrients and more alkaline foods).

Servings: 1-2
Ingredients:
- 2 beets, peeled
- 1 red apple, peeled
- 2 red bell peppers
- 2 cups of greens of your choice (for example, spinach, kale, lettuce, parsley)
- 1-inch ginger, peeled

- 1 cup coconut milk or coconut cream (natural, organic)
- 2 tablespoons of coconut oil
- 2 tablespoons of chia seeds
- Stevia to sweeten (optional)
- Half teaspoon cinnamon powder
- Half teaspoon nutmeg powder

Instructions:

1. Wash and chop the veggies.
2. Juice and add some ginger too.
3. Mix the fresh juice with coconut milk (or coconut cream, just be sure to choose coconut milk that has a thick consistency).
4. Add the cinnamon and nutmeg powder. Sweeten with stevia. Stir well.
5. Place 2 tablespoons of chia seeds on top.

You can serve it now or chill in a fridge or a couple of hours. It certainly does make a healthy, alkaline treat.

More options:

You can blend in a banana for more natural sweetness (banana is not an alkaline fruit, but it has many vital minerals, like magnesium and potassium, and you should not fear it; it's great as a non-alkaline, but still healthy part of your diet). You can even freeze it and serve it as alkaline ice cream! Yum.

You can add some nuts, like almonds. Again, don't fear calories, focus on nutrition. Almonds are rich in: Riboflavin, Vitamin E, Magnesium and Manganese. Besides, they have alkalizing properties (yes, they are among "alkaline nuts", alongside other nuts such as: flax seeds, pumpkin seeds, sesame seeds and sunflower seeds.)

You can also stir in some green barley grass powder (tastes much better than spirulina!

Additional Information:
Don't fear coconut oil or coconut milk. These are good fats. Forget about calorie counting. Focus on nutrient-dense foods that make you feel vibrant and energized.

Benefits of coconut oil:
-Coconut oil: aside from its soft, exotic taste, it has plenty of health benefits. For example, it acts as a natural antimicrobial and helps clean the bacteria out of your esophagus.
-Coconut oil is antimicrobial. Eating coconut oil helps clean the bacteria out of your esophagus. It heals the damage caused by acid reflux and kills the harmful bacteria in your gut that cause inflammation. Most alkaline experts recommend daily intake of coconut oil, as it is one of the best, natural, alkaline diet supplements. It can even help get rid of sugar cravings.

Benefits of coconut milk:

-Lactose-free, great for those with lactose intolerance or anyone wishing to embrace a healthy lifestyle. Personally, I don't understand why a human would drink cow's milk.

-Rich in natural fiber, vitamins C, E, B1, B3, B5 and B6 and minerals, including iron, selenium, sodium, calcium, magnesium and phosphorous. At the same time, it has mildly alkalizing, pH-balancing properties (while cow's milk does the opposite).

Benefits of chia seeds:

-naturally free of gluten

-rich in natural antioxidants

-great source of natural, plant-based protein (they are about 14% protein)

-rich in Calcium, Manganese, Magnesium, Phosphorus, Zinc, Vitamin B3 (Niacin), Potassium, Vitamin B1 (Thiamine) and Vitamin B2

-They may stick to your teeth, which looks lovely (original and intriguing, lol!); however, chia seeds are also available in powder (to avoid chia seed teeth look). Alternatively, having a look in the mirror after consuming chia seeds may help you also. Enjoy!

Really Easy Quick Energy Fat Burn Juice

Alkaline diet lifestyle is pretty much caffeine-free in its design. If you balance yourself with alkaline foods and drinks, you get your energy in a natural way, so you don't need to rely on caffeine.

However, personally, I believe that there is nothing wrong with an occasional cup of coffee or tea (black or green) as a treat. The problem is when you need caffeine to keep you going or when you can't crawl out of bed without it. As an ex-coffee addict, I have been there (it led me to adrenal exhaustion, not the healthiest place to hang out, lol!). The bottom line is- *balance is the key.* I know it's not easy to get off caffeine, as you may start experiencing headaches and irritability.

This is why I offer a simple, little-by-little approach. Green tea can help you make the transition. Of course, we need to remember that green tea, even though it's green, is not alkaline (not everything that is green is alkaline; for example, kiwis are not alkaline, nor are green bananas).

To dive deeper, be sure to get sign up for your bonus guides at: www.HolisticWellnessProject.com/alkaline

Luckily for us, green tea has some really great antioxidant and fat burning properties and is nothing to fear. Just use it in moderation (like all kinds of caffeine containing teas). This recipe is great if you get up early or need some extra boost. I am actually having a cup of green tea now (I usually mix it with fennel tea to create balance, fennel tea is actually alkaline and caffeine-free).

You can make this recipe on the go, and you don't even need a proper juicer. In fact, you can use a simple lemon squeezer.

You may be interested in watching my video: *An Easy Way to Make Alkaline Juices and Drinks WITHOUT a juicer* (+ a delicious recipe!) on my YouTube channel (the link below will re-direct you):
www.HolisticWellnessProject.com/youtube
(or look for "Holistic Wellness Project" on YouTube).

Servings: 1-2
Ingredients:
- 1 cup of green tea, cooled down (you can also mix green tea with some fennel tea)
- 2 grapefruits, juiced
- 1 lemon, juiced
- Optional: stevia to sweeten if needed

Instructions:

1. Mix green tea/fennel tea with grapefruit/lemon juice.
2. Add in some stevia to sweeten.
3. Enjoy your little green tea "high"!

Additional Information:

Green tea benefits:

-Better focus, concentration, and mental alertness: green tea has less caffeine than coffee, which is a good thing, as too much caffeine results in an energy clash. However, this benefit is not so much due to caffeine presence in green tea, but more because it is rich in a substance called L-theanine.

According to the Journal of Nutrition, L-theanine is an amino-acid that can increase the activity of the inhibitory neurotransmitter, GABA, which has anti-anxiety effects. Aside from that, it also helps release more dopamine (natural high!) and produce alpha waves in the brain (better concentration). L-theanine works in synergy with caffeine and has been proven effective in bettering brain function.

-Fat burn and improved metabolic rate
-Natural anti-cancer drink: according to numerous studies, green tea has powerful antioxidants that may protect against different kinds of cancer.

-Less infection and better dental health: the catechins in green tea can prevent the growth of bacteria and some viruses responsible for caries, bad breath, and infections.

To sum up, if you need some caffeine in your life, green tea is a great drink. Of course, moderation is the key!

Fennel tea benefits:

-It acts as an antispasmodic, anti-inflammatory, and antibacterial/antimicrobial as its seeds are rich in important volatile oil compounds, like anethole, fenchone and estragole

-It promotes a healthier immune system, better digestion, soothes nerves, and helps you relax, and it is fantastic for digestion (it also helps alleviate PMS and bloating).

To sum up, if I was to choose only 1 herb to take with me to a desert island, it would be fennel. No doubt about it.

(to dive deeper into alkaline teas and herbs, I warmly invite you to explore my other books in the series, such as: *Alkaline Herbs* and *Alkaline Teas)*

Green Balance Party Juice

Beginners may find it hard to juice vegetables. This is why it's OK to add some fruit for better flavor. However, we must remember that juicing high sugar fruits is not really recommended on the alkaline diet (yes, I know, I am like a broken record with that).

This is not to say you should fear fruit all together, but fruit is healthier for you when consumed as a whole or in smoothies, not juiced. You see, when you juice fruit, you get rid of all the fiber, and you create a drink that is rich in concentrated sugars (natural sugar is still sugar).

The digestion of liquids (like juice) is faster than digestion of whole, solid foods. This means - all that concentrated fructose sugar consumed in a short period of time (it only takes a few seconds to gulp it down right?) is not the best health solution. It is being digested and then absorbed much faster than if you had eaten its solid, fiber-filled counterpart (e.g. whole fruit).

This means your body will get on a quick sugar high, followed by an energy crash when it will crave something sweet. Not the ideal situation, right? Your body doesn't know if the sugar is natural or processed. Sugar is sugar.

This is why you need to focus on alkaline ingredients, and focus on juicing vegetables as the main ingredient, and only add some fruits here and there to make your juice taste better. You could also add some pulp to help the fruit juice absorb better.

Servings: 2

Ingredients:

- 4 big cucumbers, peeled
- Half cup kale
- A few broccoli florets
- Half fennel bulb
- 1 inch ginger, peeled
- 1 big, ripe pear to taste
- 1 lemon, peeled
- Half cup water, filtered, preferably alkaline

Instructions:

1. Wash and chop all the veggies.
2. Peel the cucumber, lemon and ginger.
3. Place through a juicer.
4. Add some water.
5. Stir well, drink and enjoy!

Additional Information:

Fennel bulb is not something that people usually put on their shopping list. To be honest, I only discovered it a couple of years ago (even though I have been a great fan of fennel tea and fennel essential oil). However, it's highly alkalizing and nutritious; moreover, it's inexpensive and can give your juices an incredible taste with a nice sweet flavor.

The benefits of fennel:

-Rich in potassium, vitamin A, calcium, iron, vitamin B6, magnesium, as well as phosphorus, zinc, copper, selenium, beta-carotene and manganese

-Extremely alkalizing and nourishing; because of its high calcium content, it's great for healthy bones.

Alkaline Fat Burn Anti-Inflammatory Juice

Great, natural alkaline and anti-inflammatory drink. Thanks to beets and cinnamon, it has an original and a bit of sweet-like flavor.

Beets are rich in antioxidant and anti-inflammatory phytonutrients, like betalains. Moreover, beetroot is also a diuretic, helping fight water retention, edema, and cellulite. So, if you don't like eating beets, juice them. Personally, I prefer the second option. Beet pulp is a great ingredient for pancakes, soups, tarts, curries, and stir-fries, so keep it and experiment with it.

Servings: 2-3

Ingredients:

- 1 cup baby spinach
- 1 cup kale
- 2 beets (with the leaves if possible)
- 1 cucumber, peeled
- 2 carrots, peeled, unless organic
- 2 limes, peeled
- half teaspoon powdered cinnamon
- half cup alkaline water to dilute (optional)

Instructions:

1. Wash and chop the kale, spinach, beets, carrots, limes and cucumber. You don't need to peel the cucumber/carrots if organic.
2. Juice all the ingredients.
3. Now, stir in the cinnamon powder.
4. You can dilute it in water or coconut water if you find the taste too intense.

Additional Information:

I know that many people may get put off by spinach and kale, but the beauty of juicing is that we can juice certain foods we are not that keen on eating and still enjoy all their nutritional and alkalizing benefits. Let's have a look at spinach and kale:

-Super rich source of the chlorophyll that has antioxidant and energizing properties. A chlorophyll rich diet will help prevent unhealthy food cravings, balance blood glucose, and stimulate fat digestion (so your body uses it for fuel instead of storing it).

- Rich in anti-inflammatory agents that prevent oxidative stress and inflammation

Healthy Kidneys Alkaline Juice

By adding more alkaline foods and drinks into your diet, you are stimulating natural healing. You are giving your body what it needs, so it works for you and pays you back with amazing health and energy.

As you may have realized, consistent over-acidity in the diet (sugar, fast food, junk food, too much caffeine) can lead to deterioration of the kidneys. The fastest way to nourish your body is through regular juicing, and if you are looking for a specific recipe to help take care of your kidneys, you will love this one!

Kidneys are your primary detoxification organs that work HARD all day, every day, so take care of them to start experiencing physical wellness and optimal energy like you deserve.

Servings: 1-2

Ingredients:

- Half inch turmeric root, peeled
- Half inch ginger root, peeled
- 1 red bell pepper
- 1 cup kale
- 1 cucumber, peeled
- Half cup coconut water
- Optional: 1 lime to sqeeze in

Instructions:

1. Wash and chop all the ingredients.
2. Juice and mix with coconut water.
3. For more energizing taste, squeeze in 1 lime.
4. Enjoy!

Additional Information:

If you are looking for multi-functional herbs for self-healing and don't know where to start, turmeric would be my recommendation because:

-It helps you strengthen your immune system.

-It takes care of your liver.

-It acts as a natural antioxidant.

-It possesses natural anti-inflammatory properties.

Coconut water is naturally sweet and can be a great addition to healthy, alkaline juicing.

It's very abundant in Vitamin C, Magnesium, Manganese, Potassium, and Calcium which makes it an alkaline drink (low in sugar, high in nutrients, no alcohol and no caffeine = alkaline-friendly).

Liver Lover Juice

Let's take care of our good ol' auntie liver. Let's nourish it with all it needs to keep working for us.

The combination of nutrients from the following recipe helps heal the liver, and the taste is extremely energizing and stimulating.

Servings: 2

Ingredients:
- 2 grapefruits, peeled
- 2 lemons, peeled
- 1 cup fresh parsley leaves
- Half cup water, filtered, preferably alkaline
- 2 tablespoons of Udo's Choice (you can also use cold pressed flax oil)
- 1 garlic clove, peeled
- 1 inch of fresh root ginger, peeled
- Pinch of Himalayan salt

Instructions:
1. Juice all the ingredients.
2. Add the Himalayan salt and 2 tablespoons of Udo or flax oil.
3. Stir well and enjoy!

Additional Information:

Grapefruits and lemons are one of the most alkaline fruits (even though the taste is acidic, which can be a bit confusing for beginners). It's because they are very low in sugar and high in alkaline nutrients.

Grapefruit Benefits:

-   Rich in phytonutrients called limonoids that promote the production of antioxidant enzymes. These help the liver remove the toxic compounds easier, thereby, protecting it and the liver in the process.

Lemon Benefits:

-   Also rich in limonoids, lemons take care of the liver function by strengthening liver enzymes, as well as regulating blood carbohydrate levels.

Super Buzz Body and Mind Energizing Juice

Who wants more energy? Right here, right now? Well, the energy is just in front of you!

Servings: 1-2

Ingredients:

- Half cup kale leaves
- Half cup Swiss chard
- 4 celery sticks
- 2 cucumbers, peeled
- A few broccoli florets
- 1-inch ginger, peeled
- 1-inch turmeric, peeled
- Half fennel bulb
- 1 tablespoon olive or avocado oil

Instructions:

1. Wash all the veggies.
2. Chop and juice, adding ginger and turmeric.
3. Stir in some olive or avocado oil.
4. Drink immediately.
5. Enjoy the energy!

Wake Up Maca Juice

Green, alkaline juices are natural energy boosters; however, by adding some maca powder, we can really take it to the next level!

Servings: 2-3

Ingredients:

- Half cup water cress
- 3 big tomatoes
- A few fennel slices
- 1-inch ginger, peeled
- Half cup fresh parsley leaves
- 1 lemon, peeled
- Half teaspoon of maca powder
- 1 tablespoon olive oil or avocado oil

Instructions:

1. Wash and chop all the ingredients.
2. Place through a juicer.
3. Place the juice in a tall glass and add some maca powder.
4. Add some olive or avocado oil for better absorption.

Additional Information:

Maca

This natural supplement is rich in Vitamin C, B, and E, as well as zinc, iron, calcium, magnesium, phosphorus, and amino acids. It has hormone balancing properties and acts as an aphrodisiac, both for men and women. As far as female health is concerned, maca can help alleviate menstrual cramps, as well as menopause issues (mood swings, depression, and anxiety).

Contraindications: avoid maca if pregnant or lactating. If on medication or suffering from any serious health problems, remember to contact your doctor first.

When trying maca for the first time, use no more than half a teaspoon a day and go from there. The recommended maximum intake is actually about 1 teaspoon a day. However, remember that maca acts as a stimulant. Listen to your body; sometimes less is better.

Boost Your Metabolism Juice

Small actions and consistency lead to big transformations. Focus on nutrient dense foods and try to have at least one alkaline juice a day. This recipe offers a unique taste, pH balancing properties, metabolism boosting properties, and is also great for your skin.

Servings: 1-2

Ingredients:

- 1 cup fresh spinach leaves
- 1 large grapefruit, peeled
- 1 big carrot, peeled, unless organic
- 2 celery stalks
- 1 beet, peeled
- Half teaspoon cinnamon powder
- 1-inch ginger, peeled
- A handful of fresh mint leaves
- 1 tablespoon chia seeds

Instructions:

1. Wash the spinach, mint, grapefruit, carrot, celery stalks, and beet.
2. Chop the spinach, carrot, celery, and beet.
3. Place through a juicer.
4. Add some chia seeds and stir well.

5. Drink immediately.
6. Enjoy!

Additional Information:
Chia Seeds

Did you know that chia seeds contain more Omega-3s than salmon?

As a great source of fiber, protein, good fat, calcium, manganese, magnesium, phosphorus, as well as a good source of zinc, vitamin B3 (Niacin) Potassium, Vitamin B1, and Vitamin B2 (Thiamine), they really deserve the superfood badge. OK, so what are the benefits? To make it simple, chia seeds can help you:

-Add more vital nutrients and antioxidants into your diet; hence, you will feel rejuvenated.
-Reduce or eliminate animal product consummation (chia seeds are an excellent from of protein for vegans and vegetarians).
-Lose weight in a healthy way (they will help you embrace a healthier alkaline diet and feed your body with nutrients, so you will crave less acidic foods that make you fat).
-Have healthy bones and prevent osteoporosis (you already know it's a great source of calcium).

Purple Energy Detox Juice

Beet root is extremely good for cleansing the liver and helping you enjoy more energy, naturally. This recipe is jam-packed with minerals and vital nutrients. Lemon and lime add more flavor to this juice and make it a great, refreshing drink for any time of the day.

Servings: 1-2

Ingredients:

- 4 celery stalks, with leaves
- 2 medium cucumbers, peeled
- A handful of parsley
- A handful of mint
- 1 beet root, peeled
- 1 lemon, peeled
- 1 lime, peeled
- 1 teaspoon olive oil
- Pinch of Himalayan salt

Instructions:

1. Wash and chop all the ingredients.
2. Place celery, cucumbers, parsley, mint, lime, lemon and beet root through a juicer.
3. When ready, place the juice in a juice glass or another utensil of your choice and stir in a pinch of Himalayan

salt and a bit of olive oil (or any other quality cold-pressed oil) of your choice. Oils help your body with nutrient absorption. Enjoy!

Spicy Red Bell Pepper Juice

Feeling a bit peckish between meals? Nothing to worry about. Listen to your body and give it some vital nutrients! This is what it needs. And this is why it is sending you the "Feed me; I need some awesome nutrients for energy so that I can work for you!" signals.

Servings: 1-2

Ingredients:

- 1 big red bell pepper
- 1 cucumber (peeled)
- 1 big tomato
- A few broccoli florets
- 1 big carrot (peeled, unless organic)
- 1 lime, peeled
- Half cup fresh basil leaves
- A couple of drops of Tabasco (optional)
- Pinch of Himalayan salt
- 1 tablespoon of olive oil or any other quality cold-pressed oil
- Optional: 1 tablespoon of chia seeds or chia seed powder

Instructions:

1. Wash and chop the veggies.
2. Place them through a juicer.
3. When the juice is ready, stir in some Tabasco (according to your taste preferences, but trust me, this juice is great as a spicy one), oil of your choice, Himalayan salt, and chia seeds or chia seed powder if you wish.
4. Enjoy!

Additional Information:

Sweet Peppers (orange, yellow, and red) protect your skin against sunburn and are good for the heart. They also have a nice, sweet-like taste and always make an excellent snack between meals. They are nutrient-packed as they are rich in beta carotene, vitamin C, folate, B1, B2, B3, B5, B6, vitamin E, vitamin K, iron, manganese. If you like sweeter juices and want to avoid juicing fruit (not the best thing to do anyways), start juicing sweet peppers (all except green peppers are sweet).

Basil – excellent herb that will give your juices a really nice flavor. It is a superb antiseptic, antibacterial, as well as fungicidal. Great for digestion. It is rich in beta carotene, vitamin C, folate, B1, B2, B3, B5, B6, vitamin E, copper, magnesium, potassium, iron, manganese, phosphorus, calcium, zinc, and even some omega 3. I always say there is no need to splurge on super expensive and exotic super foods. The best alkaline super foods are usually very easy to get. *(to dive deeper into alkaline herbs, I warmly invite you to explore my book "Alkaline Herbs").*

Super Detox Juice

Ok, honesty time: This juice has a really strong, earthy taste that I know not all beginners will love, but for your encouragement, it is also fairly palatable because of the carrots, lemons, and ginger.

Servings: 1-2

Ingredients:

- Half of small green cabbage
- 2 celery stalks
- 2 carrots, peeled unless organic
- A handful of fresh cilantro leaves
- 2 lemons, peeled
- 1 small beet (with greens)
- 1 fennel bulb
- 1-inch fresh ginger root, peeled
- Water (filtered, preferably alkaline), if needed

Instructions:

1. Wash and chop the veggies and other ingredients.
2. Place through the juicer.
3. Add in some water, if needed.
4. Stir well and drink immediately.
5. Enjoy!

Deliciously Alkaline Refreshing Juice

This is a great recipe for beginners. It's a nice mix of a juice and a smoothie with super refreshing properties.

Servings: 1-2

Ingredients:

- 3 carrots (peeled unless organic)
- 1 big grapefruit (peeled)
- 1 orange (peeled)
- A handful of arugula leaves
- A handful of spinach leaves
- Half cup water, filtered, preferably alkaline
- A few mint leaves to garnish

Instructions:

1. Wash and chop all the ingredients.
2. Place through a juicer.
3. Juice and add in some water if needed.
4. Garnish with fresh mint leaves and serve.
5. Enjoy!

Additional Information:

While I have made my point clear, and I do not recommend juicing fruits, this recipe is a bit different. You see, lemons and grapefruits are alkalizing fruits. Then, we use orange to taste (oranges are among neutral/mildly acidifying fruits as they contain more sugar), however we don't drink it pure, but we mix it with water and other ingredients.

This way, we obtain a delicious, moderately alkalizing drink, rich in Vitamin C. This recipe is great for beginners really and those getting used to drinking green juices.

Delicious Green Health Juice

Another Juice-Smoothie combination to make sure we get the best of it.

Servings: 2

Ingredients:

- A few fresh pineapple chunks
- 1-inch fresh ginger (peeled)
- Half cup coconut water
- 1 cup spinach leaves
- 2 cucumbers, peeled
- 1 garlic clove, peeled
- 2 tablespoons chia seeds
- Pinch of cardamom powder

Instructions:

1. First, wash and chop the spinach and cucumbers.
2. Juice them, adding 1 garlic clove and ginger.
3. Take the fresh juice and add the coconut water.
4. Mix well and transfer to a blender to blend in a few pineapple chunks (you can use a simple hand blender).
5. Stir in some cardamom powder and chia seeds.
6. Drink immediately.
7. Enjoy!

Additional Information:

Since pineapple is not considered an alkaline fruit (it does contain sugar), it's better for you to eat it as a whole fruit or blend it instead of juicing it.

However, remember that the alkaline diet is not about avoiding fruit all together. After all, fruit is a great part of a healthy and balanced diet.

Pineapples are rich in a magic enzyme called bromelain that can reduce swelling and inflammation. Because of their high fiber content, they also promote a healthy digestion.

Super Green Newbie Juice

This super alkaline and super green juice uses some spices and coconut water to seduce newbies...try it and let it seduce you.

Servings: 1-2
Ingredients:

- Half cup kale
- 1 cup baby spinach
- 1 red bell pepper
- 1 cucumber, peeled
- 4 tablespoons fresh mint
- 4 tablespoons cilantro
- Half cup coconut water

Instructions:

1. Wash and chop the kale, spinach, bell pepper, and cucumber.
2. Juice, adding some fresh mint and cilantro.
3. Stir well and mix with coconut water.
4. Stir again, serve and drink!

Crazy Color Juice with Coco Cream

This recipe uses coconut milk (or cream) that turns a strong vegetable juice into a nice, creamy and exotic experience!

Ingredients:
- Half of purple cabbage
- 1 beet, peeled
- A handful of spinach leaves
- 5 tablespoons cilantro leaves
- 1 cup coconut cream or milk
- 1-inch ginger, peeled
- Half cup blueberries (optional)
- Half teaspoon nutmeg powder
- Optional: stevia

Instructions:
1. First, wash and chop the cabbage, beet, and spinach.
2. Now juice them, adding the cilantro and ginger.
3. Mix the juice with fresh, organic coconut milk or cream.
4. Stir in nutmeg and (optional) natural stevia powder.
5. Mix well and blend in some blueberries for more nutrition and anti-inflammatory properties (you can use a simple hand blender for this step).
6. Enjoy!

Additional Information:

Purple cabbage is another common-sense, easy to get, and non-expensive alkaline super food. Great in salads and juices! It is rich in Potassium (healthy muscles and heart), Vitamin A (healthy vision and healthy liver) and Vitamin C (healthy immune system and detoxification).

On the Go Alkaline Juice

Too busy to juice today?

Use this recipe as a natural, quick "plan B" solution to still get in all the alkaline nutrients. The barley grass powder I previously recommended works great with this simple recipe.

Servings: 1

Ingredients:

- Half cup water, filtered, preferably alkaline
- 2 lemons, juiced (you can use a simple lemon sqeezer)
- 2 teaspoons of barley grass powder

Instructions:

1. Mix 2 teaspoons of barley grass with a few tablespoons of water.
2. Mix well and stir until there are no granules.
3. Now add the rest of the water and some lemon juice.
4. Drink to your health and enjoy!

Be sure to sign up for my free Alkaline Wellness newsletter to receive a free bonus guide "Alkaline Supplements" to learn more about foods like barley grass + more tips and recipes for balance and energy:

www.HolisticWellnessProject.com/alkaline

After Workout Quick Tonic Juice

The owner of the local grocery store, where I am a regular client, recently asked why I buy so much lettuce, kale, spinach and similar foods. His question was- *Do you have a big family or do you buy it only for yourself? If so, how do you manage to eat so many salads? Or what recipes do you use?* I told him about my juicing secret. It's not that I can eat heaps of kale or spinach, and it's not something I particularly crave. I just juice them! This is how the curious man got his answer.

He was kind of surprised, but I totally get it. I also found juicing greens a bit weird at first. It wasn't until I started experiencing all the health benefits (energy!) that I knew I had to make it my everyday habit.

Servings: 2
Ingredients:

- 1 cup lettuce
- 4 cucumbers, peeled
- 1-inch ginger, peeled
- 1 lime, peeled
- A handful of arugula leaves
- 1 cup coconut water

Instructions:

1. Wash and chop the lettuce and cucumber.
2. Place through your juicer.
3. Now, juice the rest of the ingredients: lime, ginger and arugula leaves.
4. Pour the fresh juice into a tall juice glass.
5. Add the coconut water.
6. Stir well again.
7. Enjoy!

Red Cabbage Carrot Healing Juice

Cabbage is a great source of sulfur, which helps purify the blood and detoxify the liver. Other alkaline ingredients add to the overall healing and wellbeing stimulating properties of this juice recipe.

Servings: 1-2

Ingredients:

- A small handful of Swiss chard leaves, chopped
- 4 small carrots (peeled, unless organic)
- Half of a small red cabbage
- Half of a fennel bulb
- A few mint leaves
- A few cilantro leaves
- 1 lime, peeled
- 2-inch turmeric, peeled
- A few tablespoons of alkaline or filtered water

Instructions:

1. Juice all the ingredients.
2. Add some water and a pinch of Himalayan salt and black pepper.
3. Stir well.
4. Enjoy!

Strong Immune System Juice

This juice is super rich in vitamin C to take care of your immune system, and thanks to its fresh citrus scent, it also energizes your body and mind. Try it when you have a bad day, it can really lift you up!

Servings: 1-2

Ingredients:

- 2 grapefruits, peeled
- 1 lemon, peeled
- A handful of arugula leaves
- A small handful of cilantro leaves
- 1-inch ginger, peeled
- 1-inch turmeric, peeled
- Half cup water, filtered, preferably alkaline
- A pinch of Himalayan salt
- A pinch of black pepper

Instructions:

1. Place all the ingredients through a juicer.
2. Mix with some water, Himalayan salt and black pepper.
3. Stir well, serve and enjoy!

Alkaline Juice Spiced Up

Originally, I wasn't too convinced about juicing radish, but ever since I discovered how, amazingly, they spice up my juices, I made them one of my top ingredients. This juice is particularly good for healthy eyesight as it is packed with Vitamin A.

Servings: 2

Ingredients:

- Half cup radish
- 2 big tomatoes
- 1 carrot (peeled, unless organic)
- A handful of mint leaves
- 2 large stalks of celery
- A handful of parsley leaves
- 1 tablespoon of olive oil
- Pinch of Himalayan salt

Instructions:

1. Wash and chop the radishes, tomatoes, carrot, celery, parsley, etc.
2. Extract juice using a juicer.
3. Place the juice in a tall juice or smoothie glass and stir in some olive oil and Himalayan salt. Stir well, drink immediately.

4. Enjoy, to your health!

Additional Information:

Radish helps to purify the blood, stimulates digestion and detoxification, and it is also a great natural remedy for sinus and respiratory system problems.

It is an excellent source of Vitamin C, Folate, Potassium, Magnesium, Copper, Calcium (especially if you keep the leaves), Vitamin B and Manganese. All these nutrients make them a really valuable super food. Make it a regular ingredient in your juices and salads or simply use them as a snack (I love it with some hummus).

Easy Celery Cucumber Juice

This recipe is full of healthy nutrients, which will boost the flushing of toxins from your body.

Servings: 1-2

Ingredients:

- 2 large stalks celery
- A few broccoli florets
- 2 cucumbers, peeled
- Half of a green apple
- Half cup parsley leaves
- Half cup mint leaves
- 1 tablespoon of avocado oil

Instructions:

1. Juice all the ingredients.
2. Stir well. Add some avocado oil and stir again.
3. Enjoy!

Alkaline Energy Anti-Cellulite Shot

This recipe will help you eliminate toxins to feel lighter and more energized. It's very refreshing too.

Servings: 1-2

Ingredients:
- Half cup mint leaves
- 1 grapefruit, peeled
- 1 lime, peeled
- Half inch ginger, peeled
- 2 cucumbers, peeled
- Half cup horsetail infusion, cooled down (use 1 tea bag per half cup water)
- Optional: stevia to sweeten

Instructions:
1. First, juice cucumbers, mint, and ginger.
2. Stir the juice and pour in lime and grapefruit juice, as well as horsetail infusion.
3. Stir again and sweeten with stevia if needed.

Additional Information:

Horsetail infusion is one of my favorite anti-cellulite and anti-water-retention herb. I love it in the summer, as it prevents the heavy legs syndrome. In simple terms, it just makes you feel lighter and more energetic.

(Too much caffeine, on the other hand, only adds to the problem of water retention, edema, cellulite and heaviness). Horsetail is also really helpful in fat burning and all kinds of cellulite battles. This is why I started experimenting and mixing it with juices. You can never go wrong with that.

Just like all herbs and herbal remedies (even "everyday healing herbs"), be sure to consult your doctor or health professional before using them. Even though horsetail is a safe herb in general, there is still not enough evidence on whether it can be used by pregnant or breastfeeding women (better stay on the safe side), and it is not safe to use by people suffering from diabetes, thiamine deficiency, and low potassium levels (hypokalemia).

Definitely contact your doctor to check if this herb is safe for you to use, in case you take any medications (even though natural).

Chlorophyll Antioxidant Juice for Optimal Energy

This recipe is full of alkaline nutrients to help you get rid of toxins. Its therapeutic properties are enhanced by liquid chlorophyll.

Servings: 1-2

Ingredients:

- 2 cucumbers, peeled and sliced
- Half cup of parsley leaves
- A handful of fresh mint leaves
- 2 inches of turmeric, peeled
- 2 tablespoons of avocado or flaxseed oil
- A few drops of liquid chlorophyll
- Himalayan salt to taste (optional)
- A pinch of black pepper

Instructions:

1. Juice all the ingredients.
2. Add in the oil, liquid chlorophyll, Himalayan salt, and black pepper.
3. Serve and enjoy!

***To learn more about recommended supplements you can use to enhance your healthy alkaline lifestyle, visit:

www.HolisticWellnessProject.com/resources

Alkaline Keto Juice with Moringa

This recipe uses good, healthy fats as well as low-sugar fruits to help you enjoy more energy, naturally, so that you no longer crave sugar or processed carbs. It also uses a bit of moringa tea, to add in more precious nutrients and help your body get back to balance.

Ingredients:
- A handful of fresh mint leaves
- 1 lime, peeled
- 1 red bell pepper
- Half inch ginger, peeled
- 2 cucumbers, peeled
- 1 cup moringa tea, cooled down (use 1 teabag per cup)
- 2 tablespoons of avocado oil

Instructions:
1. First, juice all the ingredients.
2. Combine with moringa tea.
3. Add the avocado oil and stir well.
4. Serve and enjoy!

You can also use moringa powder, instead of moringa tea. Works great if you are pressed for time.

Deep Relaxation Alkaline Juice

This delicious herbal style juice uses chamomile tea to stimulate relaxation and peace of mind.

Servings: 1-2

Ingredients:

- 1 cup chamomile infusion, cooled down a bit (use 1 teabag per cup)
- 2-inch ginger, peeled
- 4 carrots (peeled, unless organic)
- 1 lime, peeled
- 2 red bell peppers
- A handful of fresh mint leaves
- Stevia to sweeten (optional)

Instructions:

1. Juice all the ingredients.
2. Mix the juice with the chamomile infusion.
3. Stir well and add stevia for naturally sweet taste.
4. Enjoy!

Pomegranate Avocado No More Cravings Juice

Pomegranate juice is full of alkaline minerals as well as Vitamin C (pomegranate is low in sugar which makes it an alkaline fruit).

It's a natural antioxidant and anti-inflammatory. It blends really well with ginger, turmeric, and mint. Avocado oil adds in some good fats- exactly what you need to stop craving sugar and processed carbs. This juice will make you crave more of the "good stuff".

Servings: 2
Ingredients:
- 1 cup pomegranate seeds
- 1-inch ginger root, peeled
- 1-inch turmeric root, peeled
- A handful of fresh mint leaves
- A handful of arugula leaves
- 2 tablespoons of avocado oil
- Himalayan salt to taste (optional)
- Black pepper to taste (optional)

Instructions:

1. Juice the pomegranate seeds, ginger, turmeric, and mint.
2. Combine with avocado oil.
3. Serve and enjoy!

Pomegranate is one of the best alkaline fruits you can get. It's very abundant in vitamin C and vitamin E, as well as folate, potassium, and vitamin K. At the same time, it's very low in sugar, which combined with its high nutrient profile makes it a highly alkaline fruit.

Cucumber Kale Weight Loss Juice

While it's hard to eat a mountain of greens and cucumbers, it's easy to drink their juice and get all the vital nutrients from them. Make, it, drink it and forget it, right? It gets even easier if we mix our green juice with coconut water and coconut milk to create a tasty, delicious and creamy alkaline drink.

Servings: 2

Ingredients:
- 1 cup of kale leaves
- 1 cup spinach
- 1 cup coconut water
- 1 cup coconut milk
- 1 tablespoon avocado oil

Instructions:
1. Place through a juicer.
2. Pour into a big jar and combine with coconut milk and coconut water.
3. Stir well.
4. Now, add in some avocado oil.
5. Stir well again.
6. Enjoy!

Spicy Spinach Juice

While pure spinach juice can be a bit hardcore, this recipe is a bit different as it transforms into an original, spicy "shot of health". It's also great as a healthy aperitive before the main meal.

Servings: 2

Ingredients:

- 1 cup of fresh spinach leaves
- 2-inch ginger, peeled
- 2 garlic cloves, peeled
- 2 green bell peppers
- Half cup almond or coconut milk
- 1 tablespoon melted coconut oil
- Pinch of Himalayan salt
- Pinch of black pepper
- Pinch of chili
- Pinch of tabasco
- Half lime

Instructions:

1. Place all the ingredients through a juicer.
2. Extract the juice, pour it in a big glass.
3. Add in the coconut milk, stir well.

4. Now, add in the Himalayan salt, black pepper, chili and tabasco. Stir well again.

5. Add in the coconut oil, stir well.

6. Finally, squeeze in some fresh lime, stir again, serve and enjoy!

Mediterranean Herbal Antioxidant Juice

Tomato, ginger, and good oils make an excellent combination. Mediterranean spices make this juice taste delicious. This recipe offers a fantastic option to those who want to experience all the benefits of alkaline juicing, but perhaps are a bit tired of green juice recipes and need something else to fall back on.

Well, tomatoes are amazing, low-sugar, high-nutrient alkaline fruits that blend really well with healthy oils and herbs.

Servings: 2

Ingredients:

- 8 big organic tomatoes, chopped
- 2 inches of ginger, peeled
- 2 garlic cloves, peeled
- 1 tablespoon olive oil or avocado oil
- 2 tablespoons Mediterranean spices (oregano, thyme, rosemary- it's really up to you)
- Himalayan salt to taste

Instructions:

1. Juice all the ingredients using a juicer.
2. Combine with olive oil and spices.
3. Enjoy!

Minty Vitamin C Juice

This simple and mind-body nourishing juice will help you restore balance and energy through its high vitamin C content. Fresh mint makes it taste amazing, and stevia can be used as a natural sweetener (if needed).

Servings: 1-2

Ingredients:

- 1 grapefruit, peeled
- 1 lime, peeled
- 1 lemon, peeled
- A handful of fresh mint leaves
- Half cup water, filtered, preferably alkaline
- Stevia to sweeten

Instructions:

1. Juice the fruit and the mint.
2. Place in a big water jar.
3. Combine with water, stir well.
4. Add some stevia to sweeten, if needed, serve an enjoy!

Calming Sweet Dreams Juice

This simple and mind-body nourishing juice will help you sleep like a baby.

Servings: 1-2
Ingredients:

- 1 cup verbena infusion, cooled (can be a bit warm but not hot)
- Juice of 1 grapefruit
- Juice of 1 lemon
- A few mint leaves
- Stevia to sweeten

Instructions

1. First, prepare verbena infusion (use 1 tea bag per cup)
2. Add a few mint leaves to your infusion, cover and let it cool down.
3. In the meantime, extract some lemon and grapefruit juice.
4. Mix the juice with the infusion.
5. Stir well and add stevia for naturally sweet taste.
6. Enjoy!

The Amazing Health Benefits of Verbena:

-improves digestion

-strengthens the nervous system and the immune system

-gives relief for fever, colds, and flu

-stimulates relaxation and better sleep

-reduces PMS

Verbena is considered a safe herb, but there is not enough information to confirm whether it can be used during pregnancy or breast-feeding. The same applies to possible contraindications with other medications. I always recommend consulting with your doctor first.

Extra information:

Have you ever tried verbena essential oil? It is miraculous! It is definitely one of my favorite oils and a great natural way to help you relax and enjoy better sleep. I usually use it for self-massage. I mix a few drops in a tablespoon of coconut oil or other vegetable oil, and I massage my neck, shoulders, and feet. Verbena essential oil smells phenomenal...It's a great way to unwind and create your holistic spa at home.

Pomegranate Detox Nutrient Rich Water

I love this recipe in the summer. It provides freshness and hydration. It all starts on the cellular level, and your cells need optimal hydration and nutrition. This recipe provides it all and is a great alternative to sodas and artificial juices (or even homemade fruit juices made of non-alkaline fruits that are rich in sugar). Try this recipe, and for better results, drink every day and observe your energy levels. You will feel much more energized! It's also great for workouts and outdoor activities. Put it in a water bottle and place in a freezer for a couple of hours or add some ice cubes.

Servings: 4-6

Ingredients:

- 1 cup pomegranate
- 1 cucumber, peeled
- 1-inch ginger root, peeled
- 1-inch turmeric root, peeled
- Half cup mint (can be also cilantro), fresh
- 3-4 cups of water (alkaline or filtered)
- A few lime slices
- Stevia to sweeten (optional)

Instructions:

1. First, juice the pomegranate seeds, cucumber, ginger, turmeric and mint.
2. Place the juice into a water jar or pitcher.
3. Pour in 3-4 cups of water to dilute it (it all depends on taste intensity you want to achieve).
4. Add a few lime slices and some stevia to sweeten (optional).
5. Enjoy! This is a great non-alcoholic drink recipe that always gets full attention at parties and family occasions.

Additional Information:

My tip: add some ice cubes for extra freshness. You can even freeze some alkaline juices (ginger, lemon, spinach) and use them as your mega magic ice cubes. I also like to add a few drops of liquid chlorophyll for more alkalinity. However, it may put off some people, so if you want to share this recipe with more people, I suggest you try the chlorophyll option only for yourself. It does not change the taste (unless you overdose it), but many people consider a green drink (even though it smells delicious) as something weird. To sum up, implement your chlorophyll experiments slowly but steadily.
Enjoy!

Alkaline Party- Green Mojito Juice

Talking about parties and non-alcoholic beverages, you may also try this one!

Servings: 4-6

Ingredients:

- 3 cucumbers, peeled
- Half cup fresh mint leaves
- Half cup fresh basil leaves
- 2 green apples
- 2 limes, peeled
- 1 lime, sliced, to infuse and garnish
- A few mint leaves to garnish
- 3 cups alkaline (or filtered) water
- Stevia to sweeten (optional)
- A few ice cubes to serve

Ingredients:

1. Wash and chop the cucumbers, limes and apples. Deseed the apples as well.
2. Juice them, adding half cup of mint and half cup basil leaves.
3. Pour the fresh juice into a tall water jar or pitcher.
4. Add the water, lime slices and stevia.
5. Stir in well, chill in a fridge, and serve with ice cubes.

Don't forget to sign up for your bonuses and more tips, inspiration and recipes delivered to your email:

www.holisticwellnessproject.com/alkaline

3 Free Bonus Guides

CONCLUSION- GET STARTED TODAY

Take meaningful and purposeful action today. Small actions and consistency always lead to big transformations.

Promise yourself to love your beautiful body, your self-care and focus on adding an abundance of nutrients through alkaline juicing.

Create a vision of vibrant health and stick to it. Your actions can lead you closer to your vision or take you away from it. Yes, sometimes you might be tempted to get off track, bad days happen. But...remember that you can choose. You can also choose to love your beautiful mind and use it as a "navigation tool" on your journey. It's up to you what you decide to focus on. So, even if you get off track, you can choose to stop beating yourself up and re-commit to vibrant health.

Below are my extra tips and recommendations to help you create long-term, sustainable success with the alkaline diet so that you can live a healthy, balanced lifestyle you enjoy. Remember, it's not about being perfect.

It's all about progress and those small micro actions and commitments. So, in alignment with that mindset, ask yourself: "what can I do today to move closer to my wellness goals":

- Try to have at least 1 alkaline juice a day (or every other day). Smoothies are also awesome. With one smoothie and one juice a day you will succeed sooner than you think (you can check out my other books such as *Alkaline Protein Smoothies* or *Alkaline Drinks* for more recipes)

- Try to have at least 1 big raw salad a day. You can also start adding more greens to your other meals. Again, this does not mean that you should live on greens and green salads alone. But you should get in a habit of serving massive portions of leafy green veggies with your meals (You can dive into my book *Alkaline Salads* for simple salad recipe ideas, easy to implement, even on a busy schedule).

- Drink plenty of filtered alkaline water. You can purchase a water pitcher, which will help you save money in the long run. Most bottled water brands have an acidifying effect on our body. Switching to alkaline water will be the best health investment you have ever made. A good water pitcher can be ordered for less than $50.

As for any extra tools and resources, you can check the "resources" section on my website for my personal recommendations:

www.HolisticWellnessProject.com/resources

- Try to shift your diet in a more "plant-based" direction (even if you are not fully vegan, you can always try to focus more on whole-food, plant-based options). Plant-based recipes can be simple, delicious, nutritious and inexpensive.

- Reduce caffeine. As soon as you start adding more alkaline foods into your diet, your energy levels will skyrocket. By eating and drinking more alkaline, you will not be craving caffeine, and you will also enjoy more energy levels, naturally.

- Ask yourself everyday how you can add more veggies, especially raw veggies, into your diet.

- Move your body. If you are not a gym person, start going for long, revitalizing walks. Ask a friend to accompany you, if you feel like this will help you get and stay motivated. You can also combine your walks with a social life; just call a friend or create your health group via meetup.com. You can also check out "body weight workouts". I am a big fan of short, simple and effective body weight workouts I can do even on a busy schedule. I follow a lady named Betty Rocker, and I love her workouts (I got all her programs and I am in love with the benefits I am getting from following her simple body weight systems).

- Relax, practice mindfulness, and live in the NOW. Most of our "Western society" problems are nothing compared to what people in other less developed countries experience. We have everything. We should be grateful, not complaining. Mind that the alkaline diet lifestyle is not only about what you eat and drink. It's also about how you live and what you think. If you need mindset, motivation and empowerment be sure to check out my YouTube videos: (www.HolisticWellnessProject.com/videos) where, aside from sharing the recipes and lifestyle tips, I keep on "drilling" the mind-body topics. Your mind can work for you or against you, it's as simple as that. Shifting your mindset can help you make new, empowered choices and stay inspired on your journey. By knowing how to tune in your mind, your motivation will be automatic, and it will come from within you, to help you achieve your health goals and enjoy the process of your transformation.

LET'S CONNECT

1. Join my Alkaline Wellness Newsletter and get free instant access to my best tips and recipes, quick inspirational emails to help you stay on track, and everything you need to restore balance and energy through the alkaline diet & lifestyle:

   Visit the secure sign up link at:

   www.HolisticWellnessProject.com/alkaline

2. Follow my blog for more recipes, tips and resources:

   www.HolisticWellnessProject.com

3. Follow me on Social Media, to receive daily inspiration:

   Facebook: www.Facebook.com/HolisticWellnessProject

   Instagram: www.instagram.com/marta_wellness

   YouTube: www.HolisticWellnessProject.com/youtube

4. My email (in case you want to say Hi):
   info@holisticwellnessproject.com

My books, courses and recommendations:

Books: www.HolisticWellnessProject.com/books

Courses & Coaching: www.AlkalineDietLifestyle.com

My recommendations (diet, tools, supplements, natural remedies):

www.HolisticWellnessProject.com/resources

5. Follow my work on Amazon to get notified about my new book releases and massive discounts:

www.amazon.com/author/mtuchowska

Have a wonderful day, I hope we will "meet" again.
It's always an honor to create for you and share with you.

Wishing you all the best on your wellness quest,

Marta "Wellness" Tuchowska

MORE BOOKS WRITTEN BY MARTA

Available at:

www.HolisticWellnessProject.com/books

www.amazon.com/author/mtuchowska

Marta "Wellness" Tuchowska is a serial wellness author, passionate alkaline lifestyle practitioner, mindful self-care coach and certified holistic nutritionist on a mission. She wants to help you restore energy, balance and zest for life. You can learn more about Marta at: www.HolisticWellnessProject.com

Made in the USA
Middletown, DE
18 February 2020